ALASKA • YUKON

Wild
Flowers
GUIDE

ALASKA • YUKON

Wild Flowers

GUIDE

Helen A. White, Editor
Maxcine Williams, Assistant Editor
Illustrations by Virginia Howie

ALASKA NORTHWEST BOOKS™
Anchorage • Edmonds

baby's breath. Frequently we have used more than one common name for a plant in our descriptions. This is because that flower is probably of wide distribution and has been called by different names in different parts of the country. For instance, the flower most of us here know as shooting star is called bird bill and prairie pointer in other sections of the land. Try naming a few flowers to suit your own fancy.

It is not generally realized that latitude compensates for altitude in flower habitats. Many flowering plants found thriving on the Arctic coast also grow at comparatively high altitudes in the mountains of Southcentral Alaska. Some of these same plants flourish at much higher elevations in the Colorado Rockies. Roughly speaking one can find equivalent plants by climbing 200 feet or by going north one degree or about 72 miles. Also, the higher one climbs or the farther north he travels, the later will be the blooming period, as a rule.

The state is so vast and so much of it literally unexplored by botanists, that it is entirely possible that species hitherto unknown to Alaska may be discovered in years to come. Just because a certain species is not described in any published form does not mean that it cannot be found here. It means only that it has not YET been found in the state. You might be the lucky person to find a new species — or one new to Alaska at least.

A common misconception among many people is that there are no poisonous plants in Alaska. This simply is not true. Some extremely poisonous plants are found in the state. Many are only slightly poisonous. That is, eating them is not apt to be fatal but can make one miserable enough to wish he were dead. A few, such as some of the *Cicutas* in the Parsley family and certain mushrooms, are deadly. Never eat plants you are not absolutely sure are safe and don't allow children to handle plants that might possibly prove to be poisonous. The old adage "better safe than sorry" surely is applicable in the case of plants.

—The Editors

CONTENTS

ALICE PUSTER

COTTON GRASS/ ALASKA COTTON
Eriophorum species

Most noticeable in seed. To 2 feet. One to several-headed, white to russet; in peat bogs, at pool sides and damp places generally. One or another of its many species range throughout Alaska and the northern regions of the earth. They make a beautiful, lasting bouquet if picked before the seeds ripen.

Opposite page—*Eriophorum scheuchzeri.* Below—*Eriophorum chamissonis.*

ALICE PUSTER

ARUM FAMILY

SKUNK CABBAGE
Lysichiton americanum

Typical, pungent skunk-like odor. To 6 feet, 2½ inches. Swampy woods and bogs. Indigenous along northwest coast of North America from Kenai Peninsula south. Said to be a preferred food of bears.

JEAN BOONE

WILD CALLA LILY
Calla palustris

Poisonous (fruit in particular). To 16 inches. Edges of ponds and in bogs. Interior Alaska and western Yukon, and circumboreal in extent. Flower is similar in appearance to familiar calla lily although not so regal in bearing.

Overleaf — Shooting star (*Dodecatheon pulchellum*) at Eklutna Flats near the Glenn Highway, about 27 miles north of Anchorage. The yellow blossoms in the foreground are Pacific silverweed (*Potentilla egedii*) and the sword-like foliage belongs to wild iris which will follow the others into bloom. This area was inundated by high tides when the region subsided two feet or more in the 1964 earthquake but the flowers continue to bloom in all their glory. Disturbing these plants is strictly prohibited. (*Robert Tucker*)

LILY FAMILY

BEN GUILD

DEATH CAMASS/WAND LILY
Zygadenus elegans

Contains poisonous alkaloid. To 28 inches. Roadsides, grassy slopes and open aspen and cottonwood forests. Most of Alaska except Alaska Peninsula, Aleutian Islands, extreme north and Southeastern Alaska. Also ranges east and south through western Canada, the Rockies and the Midwest.

FALSE HELLEBORE
Veratrum eschscholtzii

Contains poisonous alkaloid. To 10 feet. Meadows and alpine slopes from Kodiak, Alaska Peninsula, Talkeetna Mountains, Southeastern Alaska and into western Canada and south to Oregon.

KENNETH ROBERSON

7

WILD CHIVES
Allium schoenoprasum

Edible, fresh or dried; tubular foliage. To 30 inches. Grassy meadows and alpine slopes, circumboreal except for Greenland and Iceland. A remotely related species with broad flat leaves, *A. victorialis* subspecies *platyphyllum*, is found in the westernmost Aleutian Islands and Asia.

LU LISTON

8

RICHARD REDFIELD

INDIAN RICE/CHOCOLATE LILY
Fritillaria camschatcensis

Unpleasant odor; edible bulb covered with rice-like bulblets. To 24 inches. Lowland and upland meadows. Coastal Alaska from the Aleutian Islands to northern California; northeastern coast of Siberia. Color varies from light brown to chocolate and is often striped with green.

LILY FAMILY

ALP LILY
Lloydia serotina

Purple veins. To 8 inches. Dry grassy places, rocky ledges and mountain heaths. Is found in most of alpine Alaska with the exception of western-most Aleutian Islands; western Canada, northwestern United States; north-eastern Asia westward to northeastern Europe; other scattered situations in Europe and Asia.

MAXCINE WILLIAMS

MAXCINE WILLIAMS

FALSE LILY-OF-THE-VALLEY/ DEERBERRY
Maianthemum dilitatum

Fruit a red berry. To 14 inches. Thickets, forests. Eastern Asia, including Japan; westernmost Aleutian Islands; Prince William Sound through Southeastern Alaska; south to California and Idaho.

IRIS FAMILY

ROBERT TUCKER

WILD IRIS/WILD FLAG
Iris setosa

Poisonous; varying shades of blue and purple; white specimens occur rarely. To 30 inches. Coastal meadows, subalpine areas. Bering Sea coast, Aleutian Islands and south to coastal British Columbia; eastern Asia and scattered other situations. *I. setosa interior* is a similar subspecies found in Interior Alaska.

PINK LADY'S SLIPPER
Cypripedium guttatum

Variable color, irregular blotches. To 14 inches. Open woods, meadows and hillsides. Cook Inlet area, Aleutian Islands, parts of the Interior, crossing the border into the Yukon Territory and thence into mid-Canada; much of Siberia.

ALINE STRUTZ

ALINE STRUTZ

YELLOW MOCCASIN FLOWER/ DOWNY LADY'S SLIPPER
Cypripedium calceolus

Petals curiously twisted. To 18 inches. Woods, especially swampy areas. A Yukon Territory species found in Alaska in the Haines area; ranges into the Northwest Territories and south into British Columbia, the Rockies, the Midwest including the Great Lakes region and through the New England states, and southern and eastern Canada. Also in northern Asia and Europe and in isolated other habitats.

NORTHERN LADY'S SLIPPER
Cypripedium passerinum

Fragrant and choice. To 16 inches. Boggy woods. Scattered locations throughout much of Alaska from Nome into northwest Canada. Often appearing greenish in hue; splotched with pink within the "slipper."

ALICE PUSTER

ORCHIS FAMILY

ALINE STRUTZ

ROSE-PURPLE ORCHIS
Dactylorhiza aristata

Orchis aristata of some authors. To 5 inches. Meadows from the Alaska Peninsula throughout the Aleutian Island chain, Kodiak Island, Prince William Sound near Cordova; reported from Nunivak Island; eastern Asia, including northern Japan.

FLY-SPECKED ORCHIS/ ROUND LEAF ORCHIS
Amerorchis rotundifolia

Orchis rotundifolia of some authors. Rose-colored, purple spots on white lip. To 14 inches. Damp woods through most of central Alaska and into Canada as far east as the southern tip of Greenland. Often found in conjunction with *Cypripedium passerinum.*

ALINE STRUTZ

17

KENNETH ROBERSON

BOG ORCHIS
Platanthera convallariaefolia

Habenaria or *Limnorchis* of some authors. To 39 inches. Wet meadows from Anchorage through the Aleutians and into southern Kamchatka Peninsula in Siberia.

LYNDA SEKORA

WHITE BOG ORCHID
Platanthera dilitata

Fragrant. To 48 inches. Moist meadows and bogs. Coastal from the western-most Aleutian Islands through Southeastern Alaska; inland through southern Yukon Territory and British Columbia; south and east to California and northeastern Canada. Confined to North America.

19

HELEN A. WHITE

SMALL NORTHERN BOG ORCHID
Platanthera obtusata

Lysiella obtusata or *Habenaria obtusata* of some authors. To 8 inches. Damp roadside ditches, woods. Much of Alaska except for Arctic Ocean coastal zone, Aleutian Islands, Prince William Sound area and lower portion of Southeastern Alaska; range extends southward into the American Rockies and east to northeastern Canada.

LADIES' TRESSES
Spiranthes romanzoffiana

Fragrant; flowers arranged spirally. To 18 inches. Boggy meadows and alpine areas up to 3,000 feet. Most of the state except for extreme Arctic regions and Bering Sea coast. Extends into Canada and across the northern part of the continent.

ALINE STRUTZ

ALINE STRUTZ

HEART-LEAF TWAYBLADE
Listera cordata

Greenish or dark purple flowers; heart-shaped leaves. To 7 inches. Mossy forest or meadows habitats. Near the mouth of the Yukon River, Aleutian Islands, coastal from Kodiak to Washington; inland from the Yukon Territory through the Rocky Mountains. Circumboreal. There are three other species of *Listera* in our area.

CORAL ROOT
Corallorrhiza maculata

C. mertensiana of some authors. Reddish to brownish purple. To 12 inches. Damp places among evergreen trees in Southeastern Alaska and southward to Oregon and the northern Rocky Mountains.

ROGER HOFF

MAXCINE WILLIAMS

CORAL ROOT
Corallorrhiza trifida

Root shaped like a piece of coral. To 14 inches. Boggy woods and subalpine zone. Much of Alaska except for northwest portion, Bering Sea islands, Aleutian Islands and lower part of Southeastern Alaska. Range extends into the Yukon Territory and is circumboreal. The yellowish-green color is distinctive.

FAIRY SLIPPER/CALYPSO
Calypso bulbosa

Fragrant; color variable. To 9 inches. Shady, damp woods; often on rotting wood. Scattered locations in the Matanuska Valley, the Interior, Southeastern Alaska and across the northern portion of North America except for the high Arctic; various localities in northern Asia and Europe.

MAXCINE WILLIAMS

25

PINK PLUMES/BISTORT
Polygonum bistorta ssp *plumosum*

Roots and leaves edible. To 20 inches. In meadows, bogs and alpine areas to over 6,000 feet. Much of Alaska except for Aleutian Islands and Pacific Coastal areas. Extends into northeastern Asia.

ALICE PUSTER

MAXCINE WILLIAMS

WILD RHUBARB
Polygonum alpinum
ssp. *alaskanum*

Stately plant; stems and leaves edible. To 6 feet, 8 inches. Roadsides, woods, river margins. Very common following forest fires. Bering Sea coast through Alaska to the Yukon and Northwest Territories. Indigenous to Alaska and northwest Canada. Grows in large clumps and is quite showy.

Overleaf — Pink lady's slipper (*Cypripedium guttatum*) is found growing amidst the Canadian dwarf dogwood (*Cornus canadensis*) near the Glenn Highway.
(*Aline Strutz*)

GOOSEFOOT FAMILY

STRAWBERRY SPINACH/
STRAWBERRY BLITE
Chenopodium capitatum

Most showy in fruit. To 32 inches; sprawling. River bars and other waste places. Interior and Southcentral Alaska east and south through the mountain states and to eastern Canada. The stems in fruit are lovely in flower arrangements. Also called goosefoot because of the leaf shape.

Opposite—Mountain avens (*Dryas integrifolia*), creeping willow (*Salix reticulata*) and parrya (*Parrya nudicaulis*) growing in a rock crevice near Mile 18 on the Teller Road out of Nome. (*Paul H. Leslie*)

ALASKA SPRING BEAUTY
Claytonia sarmentosa

Varies from white to rose in color. To 6 inches. Rocky slopes, alpine meadows and wet places. Most of the state including the islands of the Bering Sea except for the Aleutians. Not found in high Arctic or Southeastern Alaska. Range extends to northeastern Siberia and also into the Yukon. There are several other *claytonia* species in Alaska.

RICHARD REDFIELD

32

KENNETH ROBERSON

MOSS CAMPION/CUSHION PINK
Silene acaulis

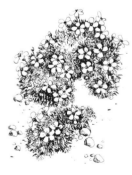

Some "cushions" reach 2 feet in diameter. Dense cushion. Sandy or rocky soil from sea level to 8,000 feet. One or the other of two similar subspecies is found over most of the state. *S. acaulis* ranges in Alaska principally in two bands; the Arctic including the Seward Peninsula and from Southeastern Alaska through the Aleutians; circumboreal except for portions of northern Asia.

MAXCINE WILLIAMS

DWARF WATER LILY
Nymphaea tetragona

White flowers, leaves floating, root-
stocks buried in mud. Edges of ponds,
and swamps. Scattered locations in
Southcentral and Southeastern
portions of the state; also scattered in
other parts of the country. More
common in Eurasia between the 40th
and 60th parallels.

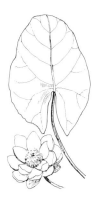

YELLOW POND LILY
Nuphar polysepalum

Roots buried in mud. Flowers and leaves floating. Ponds and slow-moving streams. Most of Alaska except the Arctic and the Bering Sea coastal regions; reaches the Arctic in the Yukon and Northwest Territories; southward through coastal contiguous United States and east to the Rockies.

KENNETH ROBERSON

35

MOUNTAIN MARIGOLD
Caltha leptosepala

Often found in running streamlets. To 16 inches. Bogs and snow flushes. Mount McKinley National Park, Alaska Peninsula; down the coast to Washington and in the Rocky Mountains nearly to Mexico. Particularly abundant in Hatcher Pass area of Talkeetna Mountains.

LU LISTON

BEN GUILD

MARSH MARIGOLD
Caltha palustris

Poisonous. Decumbent. Wet ditches, streams and other damp places. One or the other of similar subspecies is found over much of the state; down the coast to Washington; circumboreal except for Greenland.

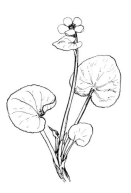

CROWFOOT FAMILY

MAXCINE WILLIAMS

WESTERN COLUMBINE
Aquilegia formosa

Shorter spurs than garden varieties. To
3 feet. Moist woods, rocky banks and
alpine meadows. From Cook Inlet area
south to California. A graceful plant. A
less attractive but very showy *Aquilegia,
A. brevistyla,* is also found in Alaska.

DWARF OR ARCTIC LARKSPUR
Delphinium brachycentrum

Poisonous; variable color from cream to deep blue. To 18 inches. Stony mountain slopes, screes and tundra. Kamchatka Peninsula and other northeastern Siberia localities; crossing the Bering Sea to the Seward Peninsula; extreme northwestern Alaska; Brooks Range; Mount McKinley National Park eastward to the Yukon. Sometimes only a few inches tall. A taller and less attractive species, *D. glaucum,* is found in much of the state.

MAXCINE WILLIAMS

MONKSHOOD
Aconitum delphinifolium

Poisonous. To 40 inches. Alpine meadows, thickets, along running water. One or another subspecies found over most of the state and northeastern Siberia. Another species, *A. maximum*, is found only on the Aleutian Islands, Kamchatka Peninsula, the Kuril Islands and Sakhalin Island off the coast of Siberia.

ROGER HOFF

YELLOW ANEMONE
Anemone richardsonii

Often mistaken for a buttercup; poisonous. To 12 inches. Meadows and snow flushes in the mountains. Most of the state except for the central Aleutian Islands; ranges into northern Canada and to Greenland's west coast.

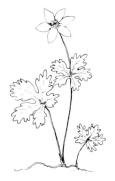

CROWFOOT FAMILY

NORTHERN ANEMONE/
WINDFLOWER
Anemone parviflora

Often found in large "drifts" or beds. To 8 inches. Meadows, stony slopes, snow flushes. Occurs over much of Alaska; through northwestern Canada and in the area around Hudson Bay; not found in certain Pacific Coast areas of the state.

NARCISSUS-FLOWERED ANEMONE
Anemone narcissiflora

Poisonous; from one to many flowers. To 24 inches. Meadows and rocky slopes from sea level to the mountains. One or more of several subspecies, often intergrading, are found in most of Alaska and extend into British Columbia. Two subspecies are found in Siberia and one in scattered alpine situations from there through Europe.

LYNDA SEKORA

CUT LEAF ANEMONE
Anemone multifida

Rose and crimson specimens occur. To 20 inches. Dry roadsides and slopes. South-central Alaska from Mount McKinley National Park and Cook Inlet area through western Canada; south to Washington and east throughout the Rockies and to the Great Lakes region. Scattered other situations in North America and in South America also.

LU LISTON

KENNETH ROBERSON

PASQUE FLOWER/WILD CROCUS
Pulsatilla patens

Anemone patens of some authors; early blooming. To 20 inches. Dry, sandy or gravelly soil such as roadsides, south-facing bluffs or steep slopes. Central Alaska, the Yukon and scattered areas in northern and midwestern North America; Siberia and Russia as well. Another subspecies extends well into Europe.

COOLEY BUTTERCUP
Ranunculus cooleyae

Petals more numerous than in other buttercups. To 12 inches. Snowbanks and flushes. Coastal from Prince William Sound to Washington. Indigenous to the area. First discovered near Juneau in 1891 by Grace Cooley, a botanist.

ESCHSCHOLTZ BUTTERCUP
Ranunculus eschscholtzii

Flowers and leaves variable. To 12 inches. Streamsides and in damp fields. Alaska Range southward, including the Aleutian Islands, adjacent Canada and the western states. A few widely scattered localities in Siberia. Many other species of buttercups exist in the state.

ALINE STRUTZ

ALINE STRUTZ

WALPOLE POPPY
Papaver walpolei

Rare; white or yellow flower; leaves leathery. To 6 inches. Loose, sandy or gravelly soil. Known only from one small area of the Seward Peninsula and across the Bering Strait in an even smaller locality in Siberia. Endemic.

BARBARA WINKLEY

PAUL H. LESLIE

PINK POPPY
Papaver alboroseum

Rare; apricot pink, occasionally white. To 6 inches. Well drained soil, preferably sandy, gravel. In Alaska known only from a few places on the Kenai Peninsula and Upper Cook Inlet until the summer of 1973 when it was found in its white form in the far western Aleutian Islands; southeastern Yukon and northern British Columbia; Kamchatka Peninsula in Siberia.

Overleaf—Alpine arnica (*Arnica alpina*), yarrow (*Achillea borealis*) and fireweed (*Epilobium angustifolium*) make a garden along the Haines Highway.
(*Maxcine Williams*)

MAXCINE WILLIAMS

ALASKA POPPY
Papaver alaskanum

Large flowered. To 12 inches. Gravelly soil. Canadian border through Alaska Range, Alaska Peninsula, Aleutian Islands and Bering Sea islands. Barely over the border into Canada. There are several other poppies in Alaska.

GOLDEN SMOKE/
GOLDEN CORYDALIS
Corydalis aurea

Annual or biennial. To 24 inches. Road shoulders and other sandy or gravelly places. Central Alaska and east and south over much of Canada and the contiguous United States. A bed of this plant in blossom does look like "golden smoke."

KENNETH ROBERSON

53

PURPLE CRESS/BITTER CRESS
Cardamine purpurea

Color varies from white to violet. To 6 inches. Moist meadows and hillsides up to 6,000 feet elevation. Most of Alaska except for the Aleutians, the Arctic coast and southern coastal areas. Also in adjacent Canada and Chukotsk Peninsula in Siberia. Many members of the mustard family are found in our area. Some are weedy plants. All are distinguished by their four petals arranged in the shape of a cross.

ALEX TATUM

RICHARD JONES

SMELOWSKIA
Smelowskia calycina

White, cream or lavender. To 8 inches. Exposed dry and gravelly areas and slopes. Brooks Range to the Bering Sea coast, south to the Yukon River and west to Siberian coast. Endemic to this area.

MAXCINE WILLIAMS

PARRYA
Parrya nudicaulis

Varies from white to pink. To 12 inches. Dry ridges, moist slopes, marshy places, arctic and alpine tundra. One or the other of the three subspecies is found in most of the state except the Aleutian Islands and Southeastern Alaska. Distribution includes adjacent Canada and Siberia.

LONG-LEAVED SUNDEW
Drosera anglica

Insectivorous. To 6 inches. Mainly peatbogs but occasionally roadside ditches. Most of the state except for the high Arctic; circumboreal in distribution, as far south as Japan and Florida. A round-leaved Sundew, *D. rotundifolia*, is also circumboreal in extent.

MAXCINE WILLIAMS

STONECROP FAMILY

ROSEROOT/KING'S CROWN
Sedum rosea ssp. *integrifolium*

Rhodiola rosea of some authors. To 18 inches. Rocky places and alpine meadows to more than 6,000 feet elevation. Most of Alaska; this, with other subspecies, is circumboreal. *S. oreganum* with yellow petals, inhabits Southeastern Alaska.

ELFRIDA NORD

PAUL H. LESLIE

ALASKA BOYKINIA/
BEAR FLOWER
Boykinia richardsonii

Favorite food of bears. To 32 inches, occasionally taller. Meadows and subalpine thickets, along running water and edges of snow fields. Endemic to Alaska and extreme northern Yukon Territory. Sometimes grows in large beds.

STEVE PRESTON

PURPLE MOUNTAIN SAXIFRAGE/
FRENCH KNOT MOSS
Saxifraga oppositifolia

Early flowering. Creeping. Damp, well drained stone crevices, rocky slopes, solifluction soil, to 8,000 feet. Much of Alaska; circumpolar in scope, extending also into Switzerland and the Pyrenees Mountains of Europe.

THYME-LEAVED SAXIFRAGE
Saxifraga serpyllifolia

Loosely tufted. To 3 inches. Dry rocky places from sea level to at least 6,000 feet elevation. Alaska Range, including the Alaska Peninsula, Brooks Range to the Bering Sea; across the border into western Canada; northern Siberia.

ALINE STRUTZ

61

YELLOW MARSH SAXIFRAGE
Saxifraga hirculis

Outstanding yellow saxifrage. To 10 inches. Mossy streamsides, bogs, meadows. Most of Alaska except for the westernmost Aleutian Islands; not found in the Prince William Sound area nor in the regions south and east through Southeastern Alaska. Interrupted circumboreal range.

MAXCINE WILLIAMS

RICHARD REDFIELD

WHIPLASH SAXIFRAGE/ SPIDER PLANT
Saxifraga flagellaris

Plantlets root at end of "whips." To 6 inches. Rocky alpine slopes from the Alaska Peninsula, Alaska Range, Brooks Range and other scattered habitats in the state; Siberia and north China. The plant *S. flagellaris* subspecies *platysepala* is circumpolar.

SAXIFRAGE FAMILY

SPOTTED SAXIFRAGE
Saxifraga bronchialis ssp *funstonii*

Loosely tufted, neat growth habit. To 6 inches. Crevices and other stony locations to at least 7,000 feet elevation. Much of alpine Alaska and nearby Canada; northeastern Siberia, Japan. *S. bronchialis* subspecies *cherlerioides* is found in the western-most Aleutians and in alpine situations on the mainland and in Siberia. *Saxifraga* means ''rock breaker.''

BROOK SAXIFRAGE/ HEART-LEAVED SAXIFRAGE
Saxifraga punctata
ssp. *nelsoniana*

Edible foliage. To 24 inches. Moist hillsides or beside running water, gravel bars. Most of Alaska except the Yukon River basin; also reaches Siberia. Other subspecies have varying ranges. One of our commonest Saxifrages.

MAXCINE WILLIAMS

65

SPIKED SAXIFRAGE
Saxifraga spicata

Petals pale greenish-yellow; leaves thick, vary from heart-shaped to oval. To 28 inches. Moist, stony slopes and streamsides; tundra. Saint Lawrence Island, Seward Peninsula, areas surrounding lower portions of the Yukon and Kuskokwim rivers and southern Brooks Range. Indigenous to the state except for one small area of the Yukon Territory.

ALINE STRUTZ

ALINE STRUTZ

NODDING OR
BULBLET SAXIFRAGE
Saxifraga cernua

Reddish bulblets in axils of stem leaves. To 12 inches. Moist alpine situations. Alaska Range, Brooks Range, Seward Peninsula, Arctic Slope, Saint Lawrence and Nunivak Islands, upper part of Southeastern Alaska, circumboreal, including Greenland and Iceland.

SAXIFRAGE FAMILY

STIFF STEM SAXIFRAGE/
RUSTY SAXIFRAGE
Saxifraga hieracifolia

Stiff, leafless stem; odd colored flowers. To 39 inches. Moist places such as snow flushes and mountain meadows and moraines. Almost circumpolar in extent; most of Alaska except for Aleutian Islands and Southeastern portion of state.

ALEX TATUM

KENNETH ROBERSON

GRASS OF PARNASSUS
Parnassia palustris

Name derived from Grecian Mount Parnassus.
To 18 inches. Moist meadows and drier
habitats, too. Most of the state except for
Kodiak Island, Alaska Peninsula, Aleutian
Islands and lower half of Southeastern
Alaska. Circumboreal except for Greenland.

ROSE FAMILY

MAXCINE WILLIAMS

LUETKEA/ALASKA SPIREA
Luetkea pectinata

Often mistaken for a saxifrage. To 6 inches. Snow flushes, streamsides and other alpine habitats. Interrupted coastal areas from Alaska Peninsula southward to Oregon; inland to Mount McKinley National Park and southern Yukon; western Canada.

GOATSBEARD
Aruncus sylvester

A. vulgaris of some authors. To 6 feet. Moist hillsides and woods, along stream margins, meadows. Pacific coastal range from Alaska Peninsula and Kodiak Island extending through Oregon; eastern Asia including Korea and Japan; scattered other situations in Asia and Europe. A handsome plant.

KENNETH ROBERSON

71

MARSH FIVEFINGER
Potentilla palustris

Peculiar brownish-purple color. To 18 inches. Along streams and river sloughs, pond margins. Most of Alaska; circumboreal. Siberian Eskimos are said to relish the leaves in tea. Our only *Potentilla* which is not yellow.

KENNETH ROBERSON

RICHARD REDFIELD

TUNDRA ROSE/
SHRUBBY CINQUEFOIL
Potentilla fruticosa

Shrub. To 3 feet. Almost any habitat, moist or arid, forest or meadow, sea level to 5,000 feet elevation. Most of Alaska except extreme Arctic, and coastal areas from the Aleutian Islands to Southeastern Alaska. Nearly circumpolar. A perfect little yellow single rose.

Overleaf—Both white and purple forms of this lovely Orchis (*Orchis aristata*) are found growing together on Attu Island in the Aleutians. (*Aline Strutz*)

MAXCINE WILLIAMS

TWO-FLOWERED CINQUEFOIL
Potentilla biflora

Basal leaves palmate. To 6 inches.
Rocky hillsides and alpine slopes. North
Yukon Territory westward through the
Brooks Range to Point Hope, Seward
Peninsula and to the Siberian peninsula
of Chukotsk; Mount McKinley National
Park and east into Yukon Territory;
scattered other locations in west
Canada and in Asia.

ONE-FLOWERED CINQUEFOIL
Potentilla uniflora

Lovely and choice. To 10 inches. Gravelly or rocky habitats along the Arctic coast, western Alaska, eastward through the Alaska Range and the Rockies, south to Montana; northeastern Siberia; a few scattered locations. There are several similar species. The "cinquefoil" in the name is misleading as this plant has only three "fingers" to its leaves instead of five.

ROBERT TUCKER

SILVERWEED
Potentilla egedii ssp. *grandis*

Potentilla anserina ssp *grandis* of some authors. Distinguished by strawberry-like runners. To 14 inches. Seashores, lakesides and along streams. All together the several subspecies of *P. egedii* are found in most of the state and are circumpolar, although somewhat interrupted. The undersides of the leaves are silvery in color. Several other *Potentilla* species exist in our area.

MAXCINE WILLIAMS

RICHARD JONES

ROSS AVENS
Geum rossii

Siberian Eskimos are said to eat the roots. To 10 inches, Snow flushes, stony dry places. Brooks and Alaska ranges, Aleutian Islands, Seward Peninsula and islands of the Bering Sea; across the Bering Strait into northeastern Siberia; extreme northern Yukon Territory.

ROSE FAMILY

GLACIER AVENS
Geum glaciale

Silky-hairy; early flowering. To 10 inches. Mainly upland dry and rocky slopes from northern Yukon Territory through the Brooks Range to the Seward Peninsula and in northern Siberia.

ALEUTIAN AVENS/LOW AVENS
Geum pentapetalum

White with yellow center. To 4 inches. Moist places in the western Aleutians and surrounding the Sea of Okhotsk in Siberia and in Japan. Limited range.

ALINE STRUTZ

YELLOW DRYAS
Dryas drummondii

Flower never opens fully. To 12 inches. Gravel bars in or near rivers. Eastern Brooks Range, central and Southcentral Alaska, Haines Highway, Glacier Bay, western Canada and the northern Rockies. Most conspicuous in fruit when it does open fully.

ALICE PUSTER

82

RICHARD REDFIELD

EIGHT-PETALED DRYAS/
MOUNTAIN AVENS
Dryas octopetala

Interesting in seed. To 6 inches. Alpine
tundra and snow flushes and northern
tundra. One or another of the three
forms of *octopetala* is found in most of
Alaska except for the valley of the
Yukon River, Aleutian Islands and
lower Southeastern Alaska; circumboreal. A similar species, *D. integrifolia,*
hybridizes with the *D. octopetala* and
has entire leaves. The mountain avens
is the official floral emblem of the
Northwest Territories in Canada.

ALINE STRUTZ

ROBERT TUCKER

NOOTKA LUPINE
Lupinus nootkatensis

Poisonous; variable color. To 4 feet. Gravel bars, dry slopes, alpine meadows. Abundant along the coast from the Aleutian Islands to British Columbia. Inland to Mount McKinley National Park. *L. arcticus* is the common northern species from Upper Cook Inlet to the Arctic coast. Where the two overlap there is often hybridizing.

PRICKLY WILD ROSE
Rosa acicularis

One of our most loved wild flowers. To 6 feet. Bogs, woods, roadsides. From the south slopes of the Brooks Range over most of the state except the Aleutian Islands and Southeastern Alaska. Interrupted circumboreal in extent. Hips (seed pods) edible and rich in vitamin C; petals also used in cookery. *R. nutkana,* a coastal species, is found from Cook Inlet to the other 48 contiguous states.

MILK VETCH
Astragalus species

Many species of milk vetch are found in Alaska. A few of them reach the Arctic; a few others exist in Southeastern Alaska. None is found in the Aleutian Islands. Flowers vary from white to yellow and purple. One species, *A. nutzotinensis*, has an interesting sickle-shaped seed pod and is known by the common name of sickle-pod milk vetch. It is found only in Alaska and adjacent Yukon Territory. Taken together the species are circumboreal; most are found in dry habitats. Some are endemic to Alaska and Yukon Territory.

ARCTIC MILK VETCH
Astragalus americanus

A. frigidus of some authors. To 36 inches. Fields, margins of streams, under aspen and spruce trees. Chugach Mountains and Alaska Range east into the Yukon Territory of Canada; also British Columbia and eastern Washington, eastward to the shore of Hudson Bay. A closely related species, *A. frigidus,* ranges into Asia and Europe.

MAXCINE WILLIAMS

HAIRY ARCTIC MILK VETCH
Astragalus umbellatus

Edible root. To 12 inches. Rocky or gravelly slopes, sandy river margins and tundra. From north Yukon Territory through the Brooks Range to the Arctic Ocean and westward to the Bering Sea, south along the coast to the Kuskokwim River area; Cape Newenham east to the Yukon; northeast Siberia.

ALPINE MILK VETCH
Astragalus alpinus

Decumbent, mat forming. To 15 inches. Grassy or gravelly hillsides to subalpine zone. Most of Alaska except Bering Sea islands and Pacific coastal strip; Yukon Territory to eastern Canada and the Rocky Mountains; northern Asia and Europe and in scattered other Eurasian locations.

KENNETH ROBERSON

BLACKISH OXYTROPE
Oxytropis nigrescens

Caespitose. To 4 inches. Dry exposed sandy or gravelly habitats. This, and its close relative, *O. pygmaea,* covers the Yukon Territory and most of Alaska except for Point Barrow area, Aleutian Islands and a coastal strip from Yakataga to Southeastern Alaska; reaches into British Columbia and barely into the Northwest Territories of Canada; northeast Asia.

OXYTROPE
Oxytropis species

Eighteen species and subspecies of oxytrope occur in Alaska. Many of these reach the Arctic but not the Aleutian Islands. Oxytropes are found only sparingly in Southeastern Alaska. Most prefer dry, alpine type habitat. They resemble the milk vetches in Alaska but their flowers rise from the base with no stem, with one exception.

Our *Astragalus* have pronounced stems and the keel of the flower is tipped by a sharp point. Most oxytropes are confined to the northwestern part of North America although many extend into Asia, less frequently into Europe, and to other North American habitats. Three species are endemic to Alaska while several are found only in Alaska and the Yukon.

NORTHERN YELLOW OXYTROPE
Oxytropis campestris

O. gracilis of some authors. To 15 inches. Dry open sandy or gravelly situations and grassy tundra. From the Northwest Territories of Canada westward through the Brooks Range, upper Yukon Valley, Alaska Range and Chugach Mountains eastward through the Yukon Territory and across the Canadian border into the northwestern states. Not present in Prince William Sound area or the lower part of Southeastern Alaska. Scattered locations in the rest of the northern hemisphere.

KENNETH ROBERSON

91

WILD SWEET PEA
Hedysarum boreale
ssp. *mackenzii*

Reportedly poisonous. To 24 inches. Dry hillsides and river bars. From the Arctic to Cook Inlet, exclusive of the Aleutian Islands, Alaska and Kenai peninsulas; inland into Canada, south as far as the border of Montana; not found in southwestern Alaska.

MAXCINE WILLIAMS

RICHARD REDFIELD

CRANESBILL/WILD GERANIUM
Geranium erianthum

Foliage resembles that of garden Geranium. To 30 inches. Roadsides, forests, tundra meadows. Mount McKinley National Park to the Bering Sea, including the Aleutian Islands and south to coastal British Columbia; eastern Asia. The seed pod has the appearance of a crane's bill before it pops open to scatter its seed.

MAXCINE WILLIAMS

TOUCH-ME-NOT
Impatiens noli-tangere

Fruit or seed pods pop or explode when ripe if touched. To 3 feet. Moist soil, often in shady places. Scattered locations south of the Yukon River, Cook Inlet area and Southeastern Alaska. These plants often grow among nettles and the leaves are said to relieve nettle sting if rubbed on the affected flesh. This, together with a related species, are circumboreal.

STREAM VIOLET/YELLOW VIOLET
Viola glabella

Flower outline round. To 12 inches. Moist woods and thickets. Coastal from Kodiak Island and Cook Inlet to northern California. Another yellow species, *V. biflora* or two-flowered violet, occurs over much of Interior Alaska from the Canadian border to the Bering Sea.

MERRITT HELFFERICH

95

ALASKA VIOLET
Viola langsdorffii

Flower squarish in outline. To 8 inches. Damp meadows, snow flushes, along streams; often in grass so tall that it reaches to 12 inches or more. In a long band between the 50th and 65th parallels of latitude in Alaska and stretching from Asiatic shores to California. A beautiful violet.

ALINE STRUTZ

GREAT SPURRED VIOLET
Viola selkirkii

Often produces cleistogamous flowers (seed pods without normal blossoms). To 5 inches. Early blooming in shady places and partial shade. A few common in northeastern portion of the United States and in Asia and Europe. Several other species of violet occur in Alaska, including a tiny white one, *V. renifolia.*

Overleaf—A beautiful natural rock garden grows Kamchatka Rhododendron (*Rhododendron camtschaticum*) on the slopes of Anvil Mountain near Nome. (*Paul H. Leslie*)

EVENING PRIMROSE FAMILY

FIREWEED/WILLOW HERB
Epilobium angustifolium

Territorial flower of the Yukon. To 9 feet. Meadows, forests, river bars, burned-over areas. Common and circumpolar; south as far as California, Texas, the Carolinas and eastward to Iceland. All parts are edible. Pink and white forms occur.

RICHARD REDFIELD

RIVER BEAUTY/
DWARF FIREWEED
Epilobium latifolium

Low and sometimes bushy. To 28 inches. River bars, hillsides and roadsides. Virtually all of the state and widespread in the rest of northern part of the continent; less so in Asia. Also found in Greenland and Iceland. Large natural beds of this flower often occur on river bars, hence the common name. Many less showy species of *epilobium* occur in Alaska.

LORNA WALMSLEY

MAXCINE WILLIAMS

Western water hemlock (*Cicuta douglasii*) roots.

WESTERN WATER HEMLOCK
Cicuta douglasii

Deadly poison, partitioned roots. To 6 feet. Margins of streams and sloughs, marshes. Coastal from Kodiak Island east and south through Southeastern Alaska; western Canada to California and east through the Rocky Mountain region.

MAXCINE WILLIAMS

MACKENZIE WATER HEMLOCK
Cicuta mackenzieana

Roots are deadly poison. To 4½ feet. Marshes, sloughs. Occurs in a block from the base of the Seward Peninsula southward to include the Alaska Peninsula, east and north into the Yukon Territory (excluding Prince William Sound area) northward to the southern slopes of the Brooks Range and thence west to the Seward Peninsula. From the Yukon it ranges into mid-Canada.

ZOLTAN GAAL

104

COW PARSNIP
Heracleum lanatum

Tall and stately plant. To 8 feet.
Woods, fields, alpine meadows.
Eastern Asia, Aleutian Islands, Seward
Peninsula east and south to California
and the Atlantic coast. Peeled stalks
edible cooked or raw.

ROGER HOFF

CANADIAN DWARF DOGWOOD/
BUNCHBERRY
Cornus canadensis

Birch and spruce forests, alpine areas up to subalpine zones. Most of the state; Yukon Territory, south and east to central California and Virginia. Not found in high arctic habitats or the Aleutians. Where *C. suecica* and *C. canadensis* ranges overlap hybridizing is common. *C. suecica* occurs in coastal areas from Bering Strait to Southeastern Alaska and also inland to Mount McKinley National Park. Another common name for *C. canadensis* is cornel.

WINTERGREEN FAMILY

PINK PYROLA/WINTERGREEN
Pyrola asarifolia

Color varies from pink to reddish. To 12
inches. Woods and lower alpine regions.
Northern Asia and North America except for
extreme Arctic. Occurs on one of the far
western Aleutian Islands. Dainty denizen of
the dry forests.

MAXCINE WILLIAMS

ALINE STRUTZ

LARGE-FLOWERED WINTERGREEN
Pyrola grandiflora

Petals white to greenish-white. To 10 inches. Dry woods and tundra and dry mountain areas. Circumpolar in the Arctic, excluding the Aleutian Islands, Kodiak Island and Alaska Peninsula. Does not occur in Southeastern Alaska. Several other species are found to occur in the state.

ALINE STRUTZ

SINGLE DELIGHT/SHY MAIDEN/WAX FLOWER
Moneses uniflora

Flower faces down, faint perfume. To 5 inches. Mossy, shady woods. Much of Alaska except for northern and western coastal areas and Arctic Alaska; circumboreal. One of our most delightful flowers.

LAPLAND ROSEBAY
Rhododendron lapponicum

Small shrub. 4 inches to 2 feet. Stony slopes in the mountains; taller specimens found in subalpine woods and muskegs. Much of the state's alpine locations and in similar situations in eastern Asia, Canada, Greenland, Norway and Lapland. Don't look for the familiar large Rhododendron shrub of the home garden.

RICHARD REDFIELD

111

KAMCHATKA RHODODENDRON
Rhododendron camtschaticum

A subshrub. To 5 inches or more. Sea level or alpine meadows. Aleutian Islands, Kodiak and on the Alaska Peninsula. *R. camtschaticum* subspecies *glandulosum* is found on the Seward Peninsula. The slopes of Anvil Mountain, near Nome, are often ablaze with color when it blossoms; very showy. *R. camtschaticum* subspecies *camtschaticum* inhabits the western portion of the Alaska Peninsula and the Aleutian Islands.

MAXCINE WILLIAMS

Rhododendron camtschaticum ssp. *glandulosum.* Drawing is *Rhododendron camtschaticum* ssp. *camtschaticum.*

RICHARD JONES

ALPINE AZALEA
Loiseleuria procumbens

Evergreen subshrub. Prostrate. Dry, acid soil in alpine situations. Found in most alpine localities in Alaska and the Yukon Territory; including the offshore islands and the Aleutians. Almost circumpolar. A charming tiny mountain plant.

MAXCINE WILLIAMS

ALEUTIAN HEATHER/ YELLOW HEATHER
Phyllodoce aleutica

Needle-like leaves. To 8 inches. Arid mountainsides and rocky habitats. Two subspecies are found from Japan throughout the Aleutian Islands, lower Yukon River valley, Kodiak Island and to northern California. Largely coastal.

ARCTIC BELL HEATHER/
LAPLAND CASSIOPE
Cassiope tetragona

Overlapping, scale-like foliage. To 12 inches. Dry alpine heaths that have plentiful winter snow cover to 6,000 feet elevation. Much of alpine Alaska except for Aleutian Islands and Southeastern Alaska. *C. mertensiana* is a somewhat similar species and occurs in Southeastern Alaska and southward to California. The first species is circumpolar.

ALINE STRUTZ

ALASKA MOSS HEATHER
Cassiope stelleriana

Moss-like foliage. To 4 inches. Alpine tundra. Prevalent in Alaskan coastal mountains southward to British Columbia; one station reported from Seward Peninsula; east Asian Islands, including Japan. Not found in Aleutian Islands except for easternmost ones. Its foliage appearance gives it the common name.

KENNETH ROBERSON

MAXCINE WILLIAMS

BOG ROSEMARY
Andromeda polifolia

Reported to be poisonous. To 10 inches. Mossy bogs and pool margins. Almost circumpolar in range, excluding the Aleutian Islands and a few arctic locales. The dainty blossoms are like upside down urns in form and are a vivid fluorescent pink in hue.

Overleaf—Campbell Creek valley, near Anchorage, is home to many flowers including this red-stemmed saxifrage (*Saxifraga lyallii*).   (*Aline Strutz*)

DIAPENSIA FAMILY

LAPLAND DIAPENSIA
Diapensia lapponica

Normally white; rarely pinkish. Dense cushions. Rocky alpine situations. Most of the state and eastern Asia. Does not occur in the Aleutian Islands and Southeastern Alaska except for one collection only in the latter. Flowers are large in comparison to the tiny evergreen leaves.

CHUKCHI PRIMROSE
Primula tschuktschorum

Variable in foliage. To 16 inches. Stream margins and other moist habitats, sometimes in pure gravel. Alaska Range and along the Bering Sea coast, some of the Aleutian Islands and northeastern Siberia.

KENNETH ROBERSON

PIXIE EYES/WEDGE-LEAVED PRIMROSE
Primula cuneifolia

Normally pink; white form occurs rarely. To 5 inches. From moist habitat to almost arid rocky situations. Aleutian Islands, Bering Sea coast, Alaska Peninsula, Talkeetna Mountains and Southeastern Alaska; northeastern Siberia. This most attractive little primrose often appears stemless when first in bloom.

MAXCINE WILLIAMS

MAXCINE WILLIAMS

NORTHERN PRIMROSE
Primula borealis

Normally lilac to pink; rarely white. To 7 inches. Grassy situations near the sea where there is plentiful snow cover in winter. Bering Sea coast and extreme Arctic Alaska and Yukon Territory; northeastern Asia. A similar and often taller species, *P. sibirica*, occurs on coast of Bering Sea and on the Yukon-Alaska border.

ALINE STRUTZ

OCHOTSK DOUGLASIA
Douglasia ochotensis

Androsace ochotensis of some authors. Dense cushion. Stony coastal or alpine slopes. Eastern Siberia, northern Alaska and the Yukon. Early blooming; flowers often hide the foliage because they literally cover the plant with bloom.

DOUGLASIA
Douglasia gormanii

Variable pink to purple. Dense cushion. Stony slopes to at least 6,000 feet elevation. Alaska Range from Mount McKinley National Park into the Yukon Territory. Rare and lovely. This species and *D. arctica* are similar to *D. ochotensis.*

RICHARD REDFIELD

125

RICHARD REDFIELD

ROCK JASMINE
Androsace chamaejasme

White petals; pink and purplish specimens occur. To 6 inches. Stony coastal and alpine slopes and mountain tundra up to 5,000 feet. More common in Alaska than elsewhere; scattered locations in the northern hemisphere. Dainty little flower of much charm; fragrant.

ELFRIDA NORD

RICHARD PROENNEKE

STAR FLOWER
Trientalis europaea
ssp. *europaea* and *arctica*

"Stars" have six or more points. To 5 inches. Woods and lower mountain elevations. The two subspecies of *T. europaea* occupy most of Alaska with the exception of the Arctic and are found mostly in shady locations. Also down the west coast of North America and in northern Europe and Asia.

FRIGID SHOOTING STAR
Dodecatheon frigidum

An alpine (usual) form of shooting star. To 16 inches. Mountain heaths and rocky slopes. Most of the state, occurs also in northeastern Siberia; does not occur in the extreme Arctic, the Aleutian Islands, Alaska Peninsula and coastal areas southward. Several other taller species inhabit Alaska as far west as Kodiak Island and the Cook Inlet area. Some are found as far south as northern California. Bird bill and prairie pointer are other common names.

GENTIAN FAMILY

ALICE PUSTER

Denali
8/97

WHITISH GENTIAN
Gentiana algida

Gentiana frigida of some authors. To 8 inches. Stony slopes and alpine meadows to 5,000 feet elevation. Mountains from the Yukon Territory through Mount McKinley National Park and the Alaska Peninsula; northward along the coast to Kotzebue Sound; in scattered locations in Asia, a few in Europe and in the Rocky Mountains. Curiously marked flower.

MAXCINE WILLIAMS

BROAD-PETALED GENTIAN
Gentiana platypetala

Our largest gentian. To 14 inches. Damp, grassy mountain slopes. Limited range; found only in coastal alpine areas from Kodiak Island to British Columbia. Brilliant blue; opens fully only in bright sunlight.

GLAUCOUS GENTIAN
Gentiana glauca

Bluish-green flower. To 6 inches. Alpine tundra and meadows. Not occurring in Aleutian Islands or lower part of Southeastern Alaska but common in appropriate habitat elsewhere in the state, including the Bering Sea islands; extends into eastern Asia in scattered locations and the Yukon and British Columbia. Several other less conspicuous gentians enjoy Alaskan habitats.

MAXCINE WILLIAMS

131

POLEMONIUM FAMILY

SIBERIAN PHLOX
Phlox sibirica

Pale to dark pink, fading to blue. Low mound or cushion. Limey, rocky hillsides, chiefly alpine areas. Brooks Range, Seward Peninsula, the Yukon; reported from the Alaska Range; various locations in Siberia.

ALINE STRUTZ

ROBERT TUCKER

TALL JACOB'S LADDER
Polemonium acutiflorum

Named for ladder-like arrangements of leaflets. To 39 inches. Usually moist situations but often found in much drier locations. Widespread in Alaska, western Canada and much of northern Asia and Europe; not found in the westernmost Aleutian Islands or in Southeastern Alaska.

133

LU LISTON

JACOB'S LADDER
Polemonium pulcherrimum

Yellow "eye" in flowers. To 12 inches. Rocky, arid situations from sea level to 5,000 feet elevation. California and Rocky Mountains north through western Canada to central Alaska; southwest through the Alaska Range, Kenai and Alaska peninsulas; Seward Peninsula. *P. boreale*, a lower growing species, occurs in the Arctic and in mountains of the state.

ARCTIC FORGET-ME-NOT
Eritrichium aretioides

Eritrichium nanum of some authors. Fragrant, yellow "eye." To 4 inches. Sandy and gravelly soil. High Arctic and mountains from Barrow on the Arctic Ocean, west and south to Nome; Alaska and Brooks ranges and the Yukon; scattered locations in Siberia.

PAUL H. LESLIE

BORAGE FAMILY

FORGET-ME-NOT
Myosotis alpestris

Myosotis sylvatica of some authors. Official state flower of Alaska. To 18 inches. Alpine meadows and along streams. Much of Alaska, the Yukon and south to Washington, Idaho and Colorado. Widespread in northeastern Asia and in scattered situations elsewhere in Asia and in Europe. Another species *Myosotis* is found in scattered areas of the state but it is an escapee from cultivation and not a true wild flower. Our wild species has fuzzy grayish-green leaves while the introduction is smooth of leaf, which is a brighter yellow-green.

PAUL H. LESLIE

ROBERT TUCKER

CHIMING BELLS/LANGUID LADY
Mertensia paniculata

Three subspecies of this graceful plant in Alaska. To 3 feet. Woods, thickets and stream margins, subalpine meadows. Central Alaska from the Bering Sea through the Yukon Territory and scattered other situations in Canada and the western contiguous United States. Does not occur in the Aleutians, the Arctic coast and Southeastern Alaska. Confined to North America.

Overleaf—The monkey flower or wild snapdragon (*Mimulus guttatus*) loves damp mossy hillsides such as this one along Turnagain Arm. (*Helen A. White*)

FIGWORT FAMILY

YUKON BEARDTONGUE
Pentstemon gormanii

Blue, pink or white fragrant flowers. To 20 inches. Arid situations, particularly alpine slopes, as high as 3,000 feet. Southeastern part of the Brooks Range, eastern Alaska Range, Saint Elias Mountains in the Yukon and northern British Columbia. Endemic to the area.

MONKEY FLOWER/ WILD SNAPDRAGON
Mimulus guttatus

Often mistaken for a snapdragon. To 28 inches. Moist, rocky roadside slopes, stream and pond margins. From the Yukon River south, including the Aleutian Islands, to California; western Europe. Another species, *M. lewisii* occurs in scattered situations in Southeastern Alaska; its flowers are bright pink.

ROBERT TUCKER

ALEUTIAN SPEEDWELL
Veronica grandiflora

Leaves hairy-sticky. To 4 inches. Rocky, gravelly places. Western Aleutian Islands and Kamchatka Peninsula in Siberia. Other species of *Veronica* in Alaska have much smaller flowers and are less conspicuous. Some are often mistaken for forget-me-nots but have four petals instead of five.

ALINE STRUTZ

MAXCINE WILLIAMS

LAGOTIS/WEASEL SNOUT
Lagotis glauca ssp *glauca*

L. glauca ssp *minor* has narrower leaves. Photo is *L. glauca* ssp *minor*; drawing is *L. glauca* ssp *glauca*. To 14 inches. Damp tundra depressions, mossy or gravelly slopes. The two subspecies between them cover most of the state and range into the Yukon Territory and both species extend the range into eastern Asia. Neither is found on the Kenai Peninsula nor in Southeastern Alaska.

COASTAL PAINTBRUSH
Castilleja unalaschcensis

Yellow bracts. To 32 inches. Lower alpine meadows. Southwest coast from the Aleutians to the upper part of Southeastern Alaska; extending slightly into the Yukon and north British Columbia. Endemic to the area.

PAINTBRUSH
Castilleja species

There are nine species of paintbrush listed for Alaska, ranging in height up to 2 feet or more. These herbs are, at least partly, parasitic on roots of other plants. The leafy bracts are more in evidence than the actual flowers and different members of the group are found in colors from red, purplish to yellow or greenish. The habitat varies from marshes to alpine areas, stony slopes, streamsides and meadows. The combined range of the various species covers most of Alaska except for the islands of the Bering Sea. The range also extends into northern Canada and the United States proper. A few species occur in Asia.

MAXCINE WILLIAMS

PAINTBRUSH
Castilleja caudata

Castilleja pallida of some authors. Color variable—greenish-yellow to red. To 2 feet. Streamsides, roadsides and alpine meadows. Most of Alaska except for the southern coastal strip; extends into northern Siberia.

ELEGANT PAINTBRUSH
Castilleja elegans

Bracts purplish; several stems branching from base. To 10 inches. Stony hillsides in the mountains to 5,000 feet. Range extends into northern Yukon and Northwest Territories.

ALEX TATUM

147

FIGWORT FAMILY

MOUNTAIN PAINTBRUSH
Castilleja parviflora

Bracts pinkish. Confined to alpine regions. To 20 inches. Mountain meadows of the coastal areas of the state from Prince William Sound to Oregon. Not present elsewhere in the hemisphere.

BUMBLE BEE FLOWER/ LOUSEWORT
Pedicularis species

There are 13 species of this family found in Alaska. One species or another inhabits all parts of the state and in some habitats several different ones occur living comfortably together. The kind of environment suitable, differs from moist meadows to dry alpine ridges. Louseworts (a sad choice of common name for such a lovely flower) grow from a few inches up to 2 feet tall in some species. The range of these fascinating plants extends into Asia, Europe and most of northern North America and can be said to be circumboreal. *Pedicularis* comes in many colors and variations, too.

MAXCINE WILLIAMS

148

ALICE PUSTER

LOUSEWORT/
BUMBLE BEE FLOWER
Pedicularis verticillata

Stem leaves in whorls. To 16 inches. Meadows, subalpine slopes. All of Alaska and western portion of Yukon Territory; north Asia and scattered European situations. Not found in most of the Aleutian Islands.

FIGWORT FAMILY

SUDETAN LOUSEWORT/ FERNWEED
Pedicularis sudetica

More or less naked stems. To 20 inches. Meadows and rocky hillsides, moist tundra. Widespread in the state; across north Canada and northern Asia. Not occurring in the valley of the Yukon River, Alaska Peninsula, Kodiak and Aleutian Islands or Southeastern Alaska.

CAPITATE LOUSEWORT
Pedicularis capitata

Color varies from cream to flesh-pink. Markedly different from others in genus. To 5 inches. Varying habitats from marshy to dry. Most of Alaska except for Yukon River basin and western Aleutian Islands. Ranges into northwestern Canada; a few scattered locations in northeast Asia.

MAXCINE WILLIAMS

FIGWORT FAMILY

OEDER'S LOUSEWORT
Pedicularis oederi

Flowers largish. To 10 inches. Snow flushes, meadows, stony slopes. Most of the state; extends into the Yukon Territory and is also found in Asia and Europe. Does not occur in Cook Inlet and Kenai Peninsula area except for one small locality and is not found in high Arctic or western Aleutians.

RICHARD REDFIELD

152

RICHARD JONES

WOOLLY LOUSEWORT
Pedicularis lanata

Extremely woolly, especially in bud; root edible. To 16 inches. Rocky areas of tundra and mountains. Most of Alaska; northern Canada to Greenland, northern Rocky Mountains, northeast Asia. Not found in western Aleutians or in areas south of the Alaska Range except for a few isolated situations.

RICHARD JONES

MAXCINE WILLIAMS

POQUE/BROOMRAPE
Boschniakia rossica

Parasitic on alder roots. To 14 inches. Under alders or where alders have been growing. Most of Alaska except for the Arctic coast, Bering Sea Islands and the Aleutian Islands. Resembles a slender pine cone in appearance; leafless. Not especially attractive but curious.

BUTTERWORT/BOG VIOLET
Pinguicula vulgaris
ssp. *macroceras*

Not a violet although sometimes mistaken for one. To 5 inches. Stream margins and other moist places; often found on tiny islets in small alpine brooks. This and another species, *P. villosa,* are found all over Alaska except for the islands of the Bering Sea. The range extends throughout the northern hemisphere but sometimes only in scattered situations. The buttery sticky foliage ensnares and digests insects.

ALINE STRUTZ

NORTHERN BEDSTRAW
Galium boreale

Sweet scented. To 39 inches. Meadows, roadsides, gravelly slopes. Most of Alaska except for extreme Arctic areas, Bering Sea islands, Aleutian Islands and lower portion of Southeastern Alaska; circumboreal. An excellent "filler" for bouquets; sometimes called Alaskan baby's breath because of its fragrance and dainty appearance.

MAXCINE WILLIAMS

MAXCINE WILLIAMS

TWINFLOWER
Linnaea borealis

Trailing, evergreen, fragrant. To 6 inches. Woods and thickets. The type subspecies along with subspecies *americana* and subspecies *longiflora* range over most of the northern hemisphere. A delicate little beauty, named in honor of Carolus Linnaeus.

VALERIAN/MOUNTAIN HELIOTROPE
Valeriana capitata

Fragrant. To 28 inches. Moist places, mountain meadows and hillsides. With *V. sitchensis,* a similar species, occurs in practically all of Alaska and extends westward on the Arctic Rim to eastern Europe. Does not inhabit the Aleutian Islands.

MOUNTAIN HAREBELL/ BLUEBELL
Campanula lasiocarpa

Excellent subject for home rock garden. To 8 inches. Dry roadsides, alpine ridges and mountain tundra. Most of Alaska and western Canada; northeastern Asia. A delightful little plant that should be better known.

ROBERT TUCKER

159

BLUEBELL FAMILY

BLUEBELLS OF SCOTLAND
Campanula rotundifolia

Round basal leaves, variable. To 20 inches. Well drained grassy habitats and rocky bluffs. Coastal areas in Alaska from Kodiak Island around the Pacific Rim to Mexico; circumboreal. Other species of the Bellflower family found in Alaska are less conspicuous.

COMPOSITE FAMILY

Members of the composite family number more than 125 which occur in our state. As the name "composite" implies, the blossom is made up of many separate flowers. *Taraxacum* (dandelion) is a good example. Composites offer a variety of color, size, form and beauty. Many are considered weeds. Only about 20 species are included here.

ALEX TATUM

GOLDENROD
Solidago multiradiata

Common and variable. To 28 inches, Poor, often rocky, soil from lowlands to subalpine zone. All of Alaska in one form or another; across North America to northeastern seaboard. Other similar and taller species occur in the state.

161

SIBERIAN ASTER
Aster sibiricus

Our commonest aster. To 15 inches. Meadows, river bars and gravelly situations. Most of Alaska; western Canada and into the Rocky Mountain states; Siberia. Not found in the western Aleutians and Southeastern Alaska. Five other species of aster occur in the state.

MAXCINE WILLIAMS

MAXCINE WILLIAMS

CUTLEAF FLEABANE
Erigeron compositus

Only fleabane with a composite or divided leaf. To 8 inches. Dry rocky places. East central Alaska, eastern Brooks Range, Point Hope area; western Canada and western United States; scattered other regions including Greenland.

Overleaf—Western columbine (*Aquilegia formosa*) and cranesbill or wild geranium (*Geranium erianthum*) flower in an alpine meadow on the road to Hatcher Pass.
(*Paul H. Leslie*)

163

MAXCINE WILLIAMS

FLEABANE
Erigeron humilis

Woolly. To 8 inches. Tundra, gravel, alpine meadows. From sea level to mountain meadows over much of the Arctic and Interior mountains, western-most Aleutians, the upper portion of Southeastern Alaska, south to the mountains of Colorado and Oregon. Another low growing fleabane, *E. purpuratus*, occurs in gravel beds and its grey-green leaves are woolly too.

ARCTIC FLEABANE
Erigeron hyperboreus

Color variable; pink, purple or white. To 5 inches. Stony solifluction soil in alpine areas. From western Yukon Territory in the upper Yukon River valley, westward through the Brooks Range to the Bering Sea and in a few other scattered situations throughout the Arctic regions of the state. Indigenous to the area.

MAXCINE WILLIAMS

RICHARD JONES

FRINGED FLEABANE
Erigeron glabellus ssp *pubescens*

Tallest branching fleabane, large flowers. To 20 inches. Dry meadows and fields. Upper Yukon valley and lower mountain slopes of that area extending southward into the Yukon Territory, northwestern Canada and down the Rocky Mountains to Mexico. Flowers may be pink, blue or white.

FLEABANE
Erigeron peregrinus

Blossom color variable; pink, white or lavender. To 24 inches. Alpine or subalpine meadows. From the Aleutian Islands southward into California and other western states; also in Mount McKinley National Park. A good cut flower.

ALASKAN FLEABANE
Erigeron caespitosus

Flower color varies. To 15 inches. Dry, exposed gravelly slopes. Northcentral Alaska from southern portion of Brooks Range, south into the Alaska Range and on into the Yukon Territory. Also in the Rocky Mountain regions and parts of western Canada and the United States.

MAXCINE WILLIAMS

ELFRIDA NORD

ARCTIC DAISY
Chrysanthemum arcticum
ssp. *polare*

A parent of the garden Chrysanthemum. To 22 inches. Seashore and
other coastal habitats. Ranges along
the coast from Point Lay on the Arctic
Ocean through Southeastern Alaska.
Absent from some of the Aleutian
Islands. Scattered habitats throughout
the north polar regions.

COMPOSITE FAMILY

ALINE STRUTZ

CHRYSANTHEMUM
Chrysanthemum integrifolium

Singly or in clumps. To 8 inches. Stony slopes, alpine tundra, gravel. Eastern Asia, across northern part of Alaska and Canada; southward through the Canadian Rockies, Canadian eastern Arctic regions.

PURPLE WORMWOOD
Artemisia globularia

Distinctive color. To 7 inches. Stony slopes and mountain areas. From easternmost Siberia, into the Brooks Range, Seward and Alaska peninsulas to Mount McKinley National Park. Limited range.

ALINE STRUTZ

COMPOSITE FAMILY

YELLOW BALL WORMWOOD
Artemisia senjavinensis

To 4 inches. Dry gravelly alpine slopes. Rocky places in seacoast area of Seward Peninsula and Chukotsk Peninsula of Siberia. Endemic.

MAXCINE WILLIAMS

174

MAXCINE WILLIAMS

NORTHERN WORMWOOD
Artemisia campestris
ssp. *borealis*

Showy, variable plant. To 28 inches. Sandy soil, arid hillsides and ridges. Scattered throughout most of Alaska and the Yukon, Alaska Peninsula; eastward to Greenland and west to Russia. Does not occur in the Aleutian Islands or other Pacific coastal areas. Aromatic.

ALICE PUSTER

FRIGID ARNICA
Arnica frigida

A. louiseana var. *frigida* of some authors. To
16 inches. Rocky or gravelly roadsides and
slopes. Most of Alaska except for the western
Alaska Peninsula, Aleutian Islands and
Southeastern Alaska. Range extends to
northwest Canada and to northeast Siberia.
One of our most common low growing
arnicas. A similar widespread species, *A.
lessingii*, is distinguished by its dark anthers
and drooping flower head.

UNALASKA ARNICA
Arnica unalaschcensis

Purple anthers. To 16 inches. Meadows. Aleutian Islands, Saint Matthew Island and the Pribilof Islands (in the Bering Sea) and Japan and the Kuriles Islands, south of Kamchatka Peninsula in Siberia. Extremely limited range.

ALINE STRUTZ

COMPOSITE FAMILY

ARNICA
Arnica latifolia

To 24 inches. Meadows from sea level to alpine situations. Kodiak Island, Cook Inlet environs, Talkeetna Mountains, Mount McKinley National Park and coastal through Southeastern Alaska; southward to Washington, Oregon and the Rocky Mountains.

LYNDA SEKORA

178

MAXCINE WILLIAMS

ALPINE ARNICA
Arnica alpina

Often several-headed per stem. To 20 inches. Dry situations from sea level to subalpine slopes. Arctic and eastern Alaska; extending as far west as Mount McKinley National Park; northern Canada to Greenland.

MASTODON FLOWER/ MARSH FLEABANE
Senecio congestus

Seed heads like miniature "dusters." To 4 feet. Moist locations, roadside ditches. Circumpolar; in most of the state except for sea coasts south of the Bering Sea. Arctic specimens are low growing.

SEABEACH SENECIO
Senecio pseudo-arnica

Coarse, luxuriant foliage. To 2 feet. Upper beaches. Along the state's beaches from Point Hope south and east to Vancouver Island in British Columbia; North America; northeast Asia. Height depends on habitat.

BLACK-TIPPED GROUNDSEL
Senecio lugens

Black-tipped bracts. To 30 inches. Various habitats. Most of Alaska except for western Alaska Peninsula, Aleutian Islands and Southeastern Alaska. Range extends into the Yukon Territory and eastern British Columbia and beyond the United States border.

MAXCINE WILLIAMS

ALICE PUSTER

NARROW-LEAF SAUSSUREA
Saussurea viscida var. *yukonensis*

Saussurea angustifolia var. *angustifolia* of some authors. Flowers resemble those of thistle. To 6 inches. Dry tundra and in the mountains to 8,000 feet. Northwest and northeast Arctic Alaska; in the Alaska Range from Mount McKinley National Park into the Yukon Territory. Possibly endemic to the region. There are three taller growing species which occur in our area.

Overleaf—Forget-me-not (*Myosotis alpestris*), our state flower together with smoothing whitlow-grass (*Draba hirta*) and arctic poppy (*Papaver lapponicum; P. radicatum* of some authors) at Point Hope. (*Aline Strutz*)

MAXCINE WILLIAMS

KAMCHATKA THISTLE
Cirsium kamtschaticum

Alaska's only native thistle. To 6 feet. Meadows on the westernmost Aleutian Islands and nowhere else in Alaska. Other thistles in Alaska have been inadvertently introduced and are not native to the state. The range of this plant extends into eastern Asia.

CUSHION HAWK'S BEARD
Crepis nana

Tiny dandelion-like flowers. Low mounds or cushions. Gravelly roadsides and similar locations. Brooks Range, Alaska Range and through the Yukon Territory southward through the Rockies as far as Idaho; two isolated situations on the Seward Peninsula; scattered other areas in North America and Asia.

ALEX TATUM

187

keep for several days if necessary. It is a good plan to carry bags of assorted sizes on your journeys and a little moss can be collected almost anywhere. Dampen it in a roadside ditch or stream and there you have a miniature makeshift greenhouse.

Certain plants such as our wild orchids, alpine forget-me-nots (*Eritrichium*) and many others should definitely not be collected except for scientific purposes. Such plants are much too rare in the world to risk changing their environment by transplanting.

It is certainly permissible to try seed, however, and it is challenging and fun too. There is not much use for the inexperienced gardener to experiment with the seed from rare species though. One reason they are so rare is because they are difficult to propagate and many of them seldom set seed. One should not be greedy about seed collecting either because nature needs many, many seeds in order to produce even a few plants. Of the many seeds that ripen, some are eaten by birds, others carried off by small animals, blown away by the wind or borne to distant places by flood waters. Perhaps out of a thousand seeds two or three may lodge in spots where they are protected and can proceed to germinate and perhaps grow to maturity.

If you are collecting seeds of more than one variety, be sure you put them in separate containers and label them. Don't trust your memory to recall what each one is when it is time to plant. Be sure too, that the seed is mature; otherwise there is no point in harvesting it. Some seeds require more than one season in which to germinate so don't disturb your seed bed if it does not produce the first year. Give it a chance. Some wild seed will stay fertile for several seasons but some won't grow unless they are planted at once. If you live in Alaska you will surely enjoy experimenting with our wild flower seeds. If you live elsewhere you are taking a chance in trying to grow them. If you gathered a few seeds while you were in the state or have a friend here who will send you some; by all means try them. There surely isn't much to lose and many people in other parts of the world have reported success in growing the more common Alaskan plants from seed.

Following is a list of some of the species that will usually grow quite well from seed:***

TALL	MEDIUM	LOW
Aquilegia	Polemonium	Saxifraga in variety
Aconitum	Dodecatheon	Cornus canadensis
Epilobium angustifolium	Epilobium latifolium	Campanula lasiocarpa
Lupinus in variety	Allium	Anemones in variety
Iris setosa	Papaver alaskanum	Papaver alboroseum
Chrysanthemum	Myosotis	Violas
Erigeron peregrinus	Arnica frigida	Erigeron compositus
Geranium	Campanula rotundifolia	Luetkea
Potentilla fruticosa	Potentilla in variety	Primula
	Ranunculus in variety	Antennaria in variety
	Fritillaria	Sedum

***Consult the index for common names of these plants. If seeds cannot be planted immediately it will probably be best to hold them under refrigeration until you can plant them.

GLOSSARY

ACUTIFLORUM—pointed petals.

ALKALOID—any of a class of nitrogenous organic bases having physiological effect on man; as strychnine, morphine.

ALPESTRIS—practically the same as alpine; applied to plants growing above timber line.

ALPINE—lofty or towering; growing above timber line.

ANTHER—the part of a plant stamen that contains the pollen.

AROMATIC—having an aroma or spicy fragrance.

AXIL—angle formed by the joining of upper side of leaf stalk or branch with a stem or other branch.

BOREALE or BOREALIS—pertaining to the north; northern.

BRACT—a modified leaf in a flower cluster.

BULBOSA—having a bulbous rootstock.

CAESPITOSE—many stems from one rootstock; growing in clumps or tufts. Also cespitose.

CAPITATE—dense clusters or heads of flowers.

CINQUEFOIL—five leaflets or "fingers."

CIRCUMBOREAL—surrounding the north; around the northern hemisphere.

CIRCUMPOLAR—surrounding a pole; in our area, the North Pole.

CLEISTOGAMOUS—having closed, self-fertilizing flowers, usually in addition to regular flowers as with some violets.

COMPOSITE—made up of separate parts; most highly developed and widely distributed plant family.

CONTIGUOUS—touching at boundary.

CORDATA or CORDATE—heart-shaped.

CUNEIFORM—wedge-shaped.

CUSHION—resembling a cushion in appearance; cushion plant.

ENDEMIC—native to a restricted area as with certain plant species.

FLAGELLARIS—having whiplike runners.

GENUS—a grouping of plants above species and below family.

GLAUCA—blueish sea-green.

HABITAT—the environment where a plant is normally found to grow.

HEATH—an open area of land grown over with coarse plants.

HEMISPHERE—half of the earth divided at the equator.

HIP—ripened fruit of the rose.

HYBRIDIZING—producing a different species by crossing or mingling of two species.

INDIGENOUS—occurring naturally in place specified; native to the place.

INSECTIVOROUS—feeding upon insects.

INTERGRADE—to merge one into another.

INTRODUCED—brought in from another region; not native to region.

MACULATA—blotched or spotted.

MORAINE—debris in various forms which has been carried along by a glacier.

MULTIFIDA—many times cleft or lobed as with some leaves.

MUSKEG—bog or marsh formed by many deposits of leaves, mosses, muck and the like.

NOMENCLATURE—system of names used to describe elements of a science.

NUDICAULIS—naked stemmed.

OCTOPETALA—eight-petaled.

PALMATE—resembling an open hand or palm in appearance.

PALUSTRIS—growing in boggy ground.

PARASITIC—obtaining life from other plants.

PARVIFLORA—small flowered.

PARVIFOLIA—small leaved.

PROCUMBENT—lying along ground.

PROSTRATE—trailing along the ground; procumbent.

PUNGENT—sharp, penetrating odor; acrid.

RANGE—the geographical area throughout which a plant or animal exists.

ROTUNDIFOLIA—round leaved.

SCREE—slanting mass of stone fragments at foot of cliff or other steep incline.

SSP—subspecies. Division of a species.

SUBALPINE—of, pertaining to, or growing in, mountain regions near but below timber line.

SUBSPECIES (ssp)—division of a species.

TUNDRA—rolling, treeless, sometimes marshy, plain.

VARIABLE—having a tendency to change; not constant.

WHORL—set of leaves on same plane and distributed around a stem in a circle; radiating from one point.

BIBLIOGRAPHY

The following books have been helpful in the preparation of this volume. While some of these are not strictly Alaskan in scope they do have enough in common with our flora to be useful. Readers who wish to pursue their study of our flowers would do well to become acquainted with these authors.

Anderson, J. P. *Flora of Alaska and Adjacent Parts of Canada.* Ames, Iowa: Iowa State University Press, 1959.

Heller, Christine. *Wild Flowers of Alaska.* Portland, Oregon: Graphic Arts Center, 1966.

Hulten, Eric. *Flora of Alaska and Neighboring Territories.* Stanford, California: Stanford University Press, 1968.

Polunin, Nicholas. *Circumpolar Arctic Flora.* Oxford, England: Oxford at the Clarendon Press, 1959.

Potter, Louise. *Roadside Flowers of Alaska.* Hanover, New Hampshire: Privately printed, 1963.

——————. *Wild Flowers Along Mt. McKinley Park Road.* Hanover, New Hampshire: Privately printed, 1969.

Sharples, Ada White. *Alaska Wild Flowers.* Stanford, California: Stanford University Press, 1958.

Viereck, Leslie A. and Little, Elbert L. *Alaska Trees and Shrubs.* Washington, D. C.: Forest Service, United States Department of Agriculture, 1972.

Wiggins, Ira L. and Thomas, John Hunter. *A Flora of the Alaskan Arctic Slope.* Toronto, Canada: University of Toronto Press, 1962.

OTHER INTERESTING READING ON THE SUBJECTS OF ALPINE AND NORTHERN FLORA:

Barker, Frank. *The Cream of Alpines.* Edinburgh, Scotland: Thomas Nelson and Sons Ltd., 1958.

Gjaerevoll, Olav and Jorgensen, Reidar. *Fjellflora.* Color pictures by Dagny Tande Lid. Trondheim, Norway: F. Bruns Bokhandels Forlag, 1952.

Pesman, M. Walter. *Meet the Natives,* 5th edition. Denver: Smith-Brooks Printing Company, 1952.

Schroter, Prof. Dr. C. *Alpine Flora,* 28th edition. Zurich, Switzerland: Raustein Verlag Zurich.

Smarda, Jan and Stolfa, Vojtech. *Kvety Tatier.* Bratislava, Czechoslovakia: Vydavatelstvo Osveta, 1963.

INDEX BY

FAMILY NAMES

INDEX BY FAMILY NAMES

INDEX BY FAMILY NAMES

INDEX BY FAMILY NAMES

INDEX BY FAMILY NAMES

INDEX BY BOTANICAL NAMES

INDEX BY COMMON NAMES

211

INDEX BY COMMON NAMES

INDEX BY COMMON NAMES